HURRICANE
ON ITS WAY!

Eduardo Aparicio

Rigby

To Vivian and Rebecca

© 1997 by Rigby,
a division of Reed Elsevier Inc.
1000 Hart Rd.
Barrington, IL 60010-2627

04 03 02 01 00
10 9 8 7 6 5

Printed in Singapore

ISBN 0-7635-3232-0

Illustration Credit

8–9 Roberta Polfus

Photo Credits

All photography by Eduardo Aparicio except:

cover background Bill Morson/Gamma Liaison

1 right, 21 David Spielman/Gamma Liaison

2, 18–19 PHOTRI

3–24 border NASA

4 Gamma Liaison

5 top, bottom T. Savino/Gamma Liaison

7 S. Dooley/Gamma Liaison

10 top Lixion Avila

10 bottom UPI/Corbis-Bettmann

13 bottom Lixion Avila

15 The Image Bank

17 top, bottom NASA

20 courtesy of WSCV Channel 51 Telemundo

Welcome to the National Hurricane Center in Miami, Florida! My name is Lixion Avila.

I'm a meteorologist, a scientist who studies the weather. I specialize in hurricanes. Hurricanes are the biggest storms in the world. The rain and strong winds of a hurricane can destroy homes and flood entire towns. My job is to tell people when a hurricane is coming so they won't get hurt.

This is what a Miami neighborhood looked like in 1992 after it was hit by hurricane Andrew. The fierce winds and heavy rains crushed houses and scattered people's belongings. Andrew's winds were as strong as 145 miles per hour. That's about three times as fast as some of the cars on the highway.

Imagine how strong the wind must have been to uproot a tree as big as this one! Think about the strong wind that blew the roof off this house!

It was even able to pick up this car and set it down on top of a wall!

Wind is air that moves from one place to another. In a hurricane, air moves quickly. Even when there are no hurricanes, the air around us is moving all the time—swirling, blowing, sinking, and rising. In the summer months of June and July, the air gets warm, and the ocean gets warm, too. Some of the warm water from the ocean rises like steam, forming clouds up in the sky.

All clouds are made of tiny drops of water. You've seen small, white clouds up in the sky. You've also seen clouds that are big and dark. These darker clouds are made of a lot of water and produce storms.

clouds form

warm, moist air rises

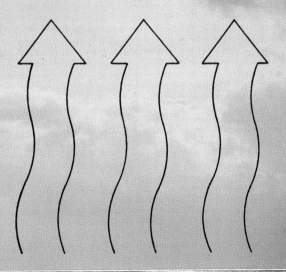

In August the air gets even warmer than in June and July. The warm wind can blow clouds over the ocean and push many of them together. With the warmer weather, even more water rises from the ocean to form storm clouds.

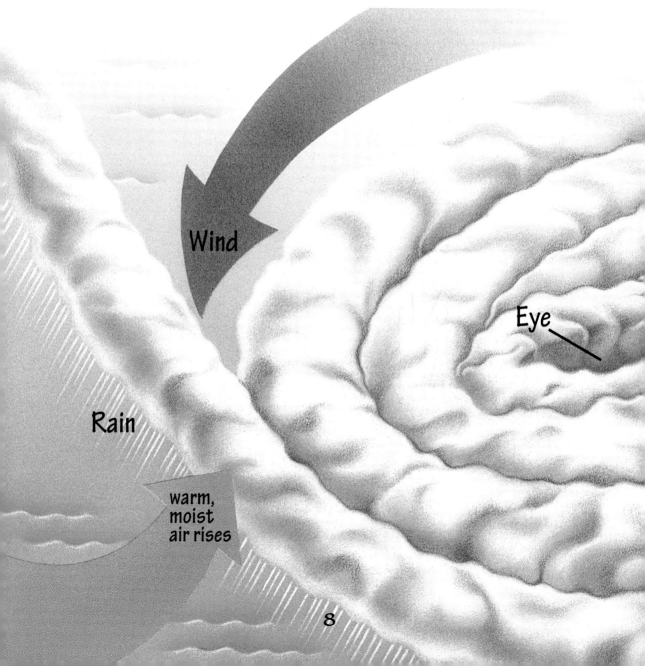

Wind

Eye

Rain

warm,
moist
air rises

As more and more clouds are clustered together, the wind makes them start spinning. While spinning, this cluster of clouds picks up even more water from the ocean. A hurricane is born!

A hurricane is a very large mass of whirling clouds. It brings strong winds and heavy rains that have the power to destroy homes and harm people.

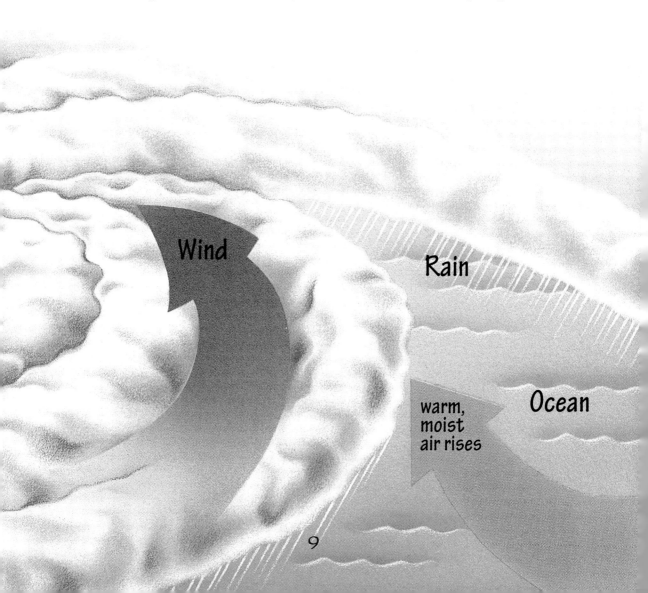

Wind

Rain

Ocean

warm,
moist
air rises

I learned about hurricanes when I was a child. Here I am with my mother and sister in Cuba, where I was born. Cuba is very close to Florida. When I was very young, hurricane Alma hit Cuba. You can see how high Alma's winds pushed the ocean's waves!

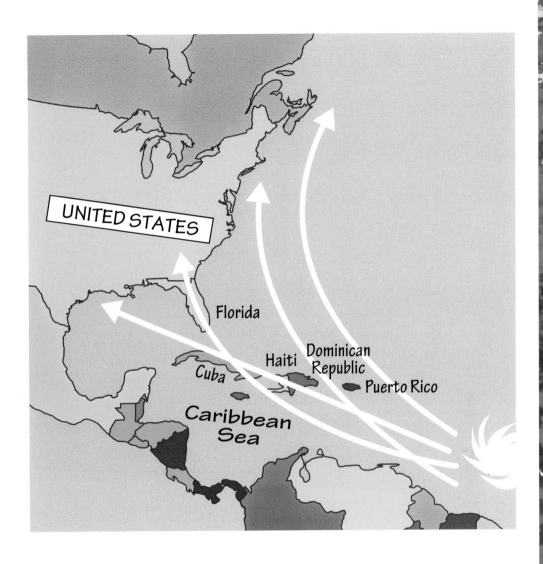

Very often, the same hurricane threatens different areas of land. A hurricane that strikes Cuba might first damage other places in the Caribbean, like Puerto Rico, the Dominican Republic, and Haiti. Then it might go on to Florida and other states along the East Coast of the United States.

In 1978 when I came to the United States, I was already a hurricane scientist. I started working at the National Hurricane Center. At the same time, I went back to school to learn more about hurricanes. In addition to taking courses about the weather, I had to take math, physics, and computer science.

Because many people in Florida speak Spanish, as we did in Cuba, I was chosen to give hurricane reports in Spanish over radio and TV. I continue to do that today. I also prepare reports and go to meetings with other weather scientists all over the U.S. and other parts of the world. That way, we share what we know and help each other do a better job.

My main job at the National Hurricane Center is to warn people when a hurricane is coming. I have learned how to tell when a hurricane is forming and where it will go. Then I can warn people so they have time to prepare for the storm or leave the area.

I work the hardest during the summer. That's because several hurricanes can form at the same time. When that happens, how do people know which hurricane is which? We give them names. The first hurricane of the season gets a name beginning with "A." The next one begins with "B" and so on. We switch between a boy's name and a girl's name for each hurricane. Some of the names used are Alberto, Debby, Juan, Nadine, Noel, and Paloma. The name can be in English, Spanish, Dutch, or French because many hurricanes form in the Caribbean, where all these different languages are spoken.

Paloma

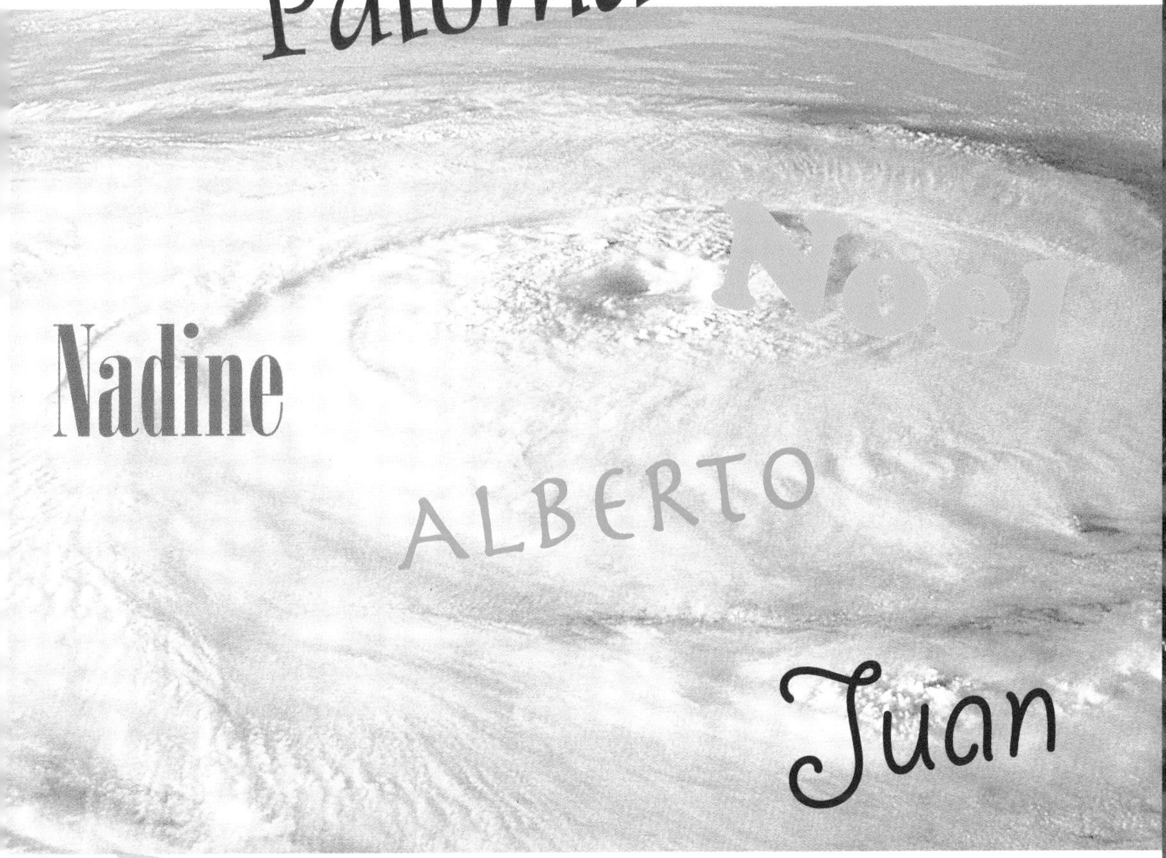

Noel

Nadine

ALBERTO

Juan

DEBBY

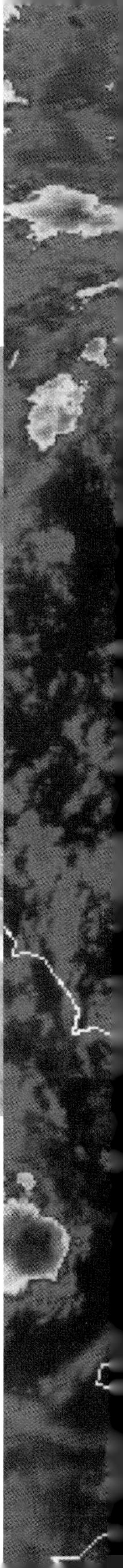

15

To predict when a hurricane will form, how strong it will be, and where it will go takes a lot of teamwork. I can't do the job just by myself. Many other scientists help me get the information I need. We feed this information into computers that help us make our predictions.

For instance, our computers have pictures of hurricanes that were taken from high above the earth. These pictures are taken from weather satellites, which are weather stations moving in space around the earth. We study many of these pictures to see where the hurricane is going.

The center of the hurricane is called the eye of the storm. The eye is a calm, dry area, but the storm rages all around it. Imagine flying a plane through the storm right into the eye. Some specially trained Air Force crews do just that! They have planes called Hurricane Hunters that are built to withstand strong winds.

Inside the hurricane, the crew uses special instruments to find out a lot more about the hurricane. They measure things like wind speed, temperature, and how much water the storm carries. They radio this information back to us so we can study it and tell people where the hurricane is headed.

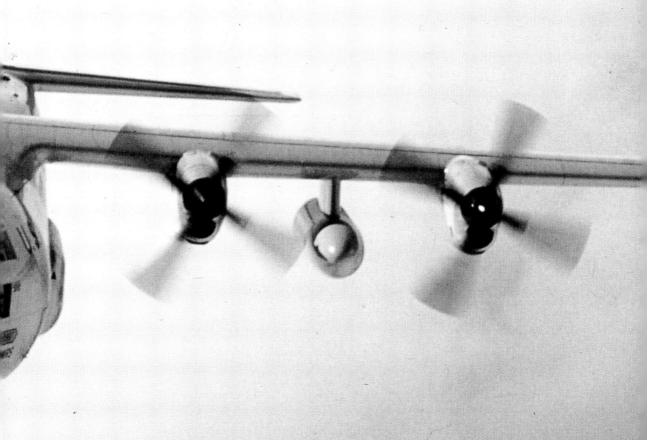

When a hurricane is headed toward Miami, I get on TV and radio and warn people. If I know that a hurricane is approaching and might hit land, I give a HURRICANE WATCH. That means people should stay tuned to the radio and TV in case I need to give them more instructions.

If it looks like the hurricane will hit the area within 24 hours, I provide a HURRICANE WARNING. Sometimes people in some areas are told to leave their homes and seek shelter in a safe place. This is how lives are saved. They can also try to save their homes by boarding up windows.

People may not have to leave their homes if the hurricane is not strong enough. But even a mild hurricane is dangerous. However, if you get ready for the storm, you'll be okay. One of the things you need to have is a radio that runs on batteries. Sometimes hurricane winds blow down power lines, and the electricity goes out. If you have a battery radio, you can still listen to my instructions and know what to do.

If the electricity goes out, you won't be able to store food in the refrigerator. So you'll need food that comes in cans and boxes and that doesn't need to be kept in a refrigerator. Without electricity, the pumps that carry water to the homes won't work, so make sure you save bottles of drinking water before a hurricane.

You have to put away everything in the yard, like chairs and potted plants. Strong winds can lift those things in the air and crash them against your home. Glass windows and doors need to be boarded up. Glass is cross-taped so that if it breaks, the shattered pieces won't fly away and hurt people. And one more thing, during a hurricane, stay away from windows and doors. The safest place to be is in a closet, hallway, or room away from outside walls.

Fortunately, hurricanes don't come that often. Today we're having a beautiful day. The weather is calm and peaceful. Most days in Florida are this nice—not like that awful day when hurricane Andrew hit Miami!

I'll keep working, looking out for hurricanes. And if I see one coming, I'll let people know with plenty of time so that they can protect themselves. That's my job. But for now, let's enjoy the nice weather!